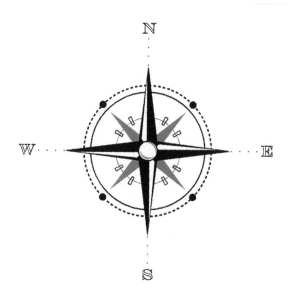

Master of the Sky and Sea

The Story of Ted Wells

Master of the Sky and Sea: The Story of Ted Wells
by James Rix

We gratefully acknowledge and thank these photo sources: Private collections of James Rix and Mary Ann Rix, NASA (History.nasa.gov), Wichita Photo Archives, Cliff Snellings, vintageairphotos.blogspot.com, Omaha Newspaper, State Archives NSW, San Diego Air and Space Museum, Jerry Impellezerri, WSU Special Collections, thisdayinaviation.com, aviastar.org, oldmachinepress.com, Wikimedia commons, Tim Vickers, Edward H, Phillips Collection, Kansas Aviation Museum, Aerofiles.com, Wikipedia, Beech Log, U.S Air Force, Tom Fey, spacebattles.com, Snipe Bulletin, Snipe Class International Racing Assoc., US Navy National Museum of Naval Aviation, Wichita State Univ. Libraries, Snipe Class International Racing Assoc., Smithsonian Institution's National Air and Space Museum, and Texas Week.

Published by Relentlessly Creative Books

http://relentlesslycreativebooks.com/

books@relentlesslycreative.com

303-317-2200

Master of the Sky and Sea

The Story of Ted Wells

Contents

Forward 1

Acknowledgements 3

Aviation Beginnings 5

History of NACA 7

Aircraft Boom in Wichita 11

Creation of Travel Air 13

Travel Air Model 5000 15

Ted Wells Early Years 17

Model R 24

Model 16 32

Model W4B 33

Beech Aircraft 36

Model 17 37

Model 18 45

XA-38 48

A-26 Wings 50

Bonanza 51

T-34 53

Model 34 "Twin-Quad" 54

The Model 50 Twin Bonanza 57

Variants Models 55, 56, & 58 Baron,

Model 95 Travel Air 57

Sailing 58

The Snipe Class 65

First World Championships 69

More National and World Championships 74

Eddie Williams 78

Rules 79

Pranks 87

Wichita Sailing Club 88

Work Conflicts 94

Final Chapter 99

About the Author 104

About Relentlessly Creative Books 105

End Notes 106

Forward

As an early and highly successful airplane designer and co-founder of Beech Aircraft, Ted Well's place in aeronautics history is assured. However, this story doesn't just follow Ted's amazing pioneering aircraft career and accomplishments, but also his remarkable success as a sailor.

This book provides an overview of many of the aircraft produced by Beech Aircraft, but this isn't a book just about airplanes. There are plenty of those around. This is a story about a man who was passionate about airplanes. His innovative designs and creative vision were so much a part of aviation history that his breakthrough biplane design, the Staggerwing, shown on the cover of this book, hangs in the Smithsonian Institution's National Air and Space Museum in Washington D.C.

Ted was closely involved in the development of so many aircraft, it is impossible to tell the story of his life without showing many of the projects he was directly involved in. These will show connections between the many facets surrounding aircraft development during Ted's life that played a part in his pursuit of designing the best airplanes of the day. Readers will also find that both people and manufacturing facilities were often connected in interesting ways.

While the airplanes produced by Beech Aircraft show Ted's ability to develop great airplane designs, it is the sailing stories where readers will get a better understanding of Ted's character. The world of sailboat racing, where Ted acquired the nickname "Mr. Snipe" after the class of boats he captained, is where we can best see Ted as a person and not just a historic figure.

Some of these stories were picked up from the tales I've heard over the 30 years I've worked at Beech Aircraft and from within the sailing communities where I sailed both with and against Ted Wells. Hopefully, when you've finished reading this story, it will be apparent that much of the company's success was the combination of Walter Beech's vision of the future airplane market and Ted Well's brilliance and innovation as a designer.

James Rix

Acknowledgements

Thanks to Dré from http://beech17.net for providing much of Ted Well's reference material.

Thanks to David Robbins and the Wichita Aircraft Museum for sharing resources and the restoration project underway of the Model 17.

Thanks to Kathy Fisher for recounting the story of her father-in-law's involvement in the Model 34 crash.

Thanks to Edward Phillips and Wichita State University Special Collections for sharing archives and interviews with Ted before his passing.

A very special thanks to my mother, Mary Ann Rix, for collecting sailing club archives and Ted Wells memorabilia including items from Ted's estate after he passed away. This book certainly wouldn't have been possible without the loads of information she has gathered over the years.

…and tremendous thanks to my wife Kimberly for her patience with me as I took on the endeavor of putting this book together.

Aviation Beginnings

At the beginning, a lot of innovation happened in aviation in just a few short years. Aircraft design advanced at a remarkable rate after the development of the internal combustion engine provided sufficient horsepower at a weight that was light enough to get flying machines airborne. Hiram Maxim, inventor of the machine gun, actually built an airplane that was steam-powered prior to the Wright brothers' first flight. It was a massive machine to accommodate the size and weight of the steam engine.

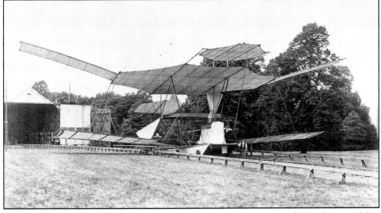

Photo taken in 1894

Hiram Maxim's flying machine

However, it really does not compare—at least in the same category as the Wright brothers' first flight—because it had no flight control system. It traveled on rails that confined it to only lift a few inches above the ground. It did, however, produce enough lift to break out of the constraining track where it subsequently crashed.

Photo taken in 1874

Maxim with his steam powered engine

The Wright brothers with the help of Charlie Taylor, their bicycle shop assistant, designed and built their own engine with just enough horsepower necessary for their historic flight in 1903. Gasoline engines at the time were not readily available and had significantly low power-to-weight ratios. The Wright brothers calculated that eight horsepower was sufficient to get their craft airborne. Fortunately, their engine actually produced somewhere between 12 and 16 horsepower, which ended up being barely enough for their first three flights. The Wright brothers deserve all the credit for "first flight" as they had solved the challenges not just of how to get an airplane into the air, but the real problem of how to control it once airborne.

A few years earlier, Samuel Pierpont Langley had nearly wrested the honor for himself. He had a more than capable engine and the financial support to build an elaborate flying machine, but he didn't have the practical experience and knowledge the Wright brothers had gained from their glider experiments. A complex design with less progressive experimentation and development was bound to fail. Ultimately his machine snagged a launch-system guy wire on the houseboat it was to launch from sending it plunging into the lake.

Once the Wright brothers demonstrated successful flights, along with continued advancements in engine design, it was easier for others to jump on the airplane bandwagon. The Wright brothers, having mastered flying and refining their airplane design, formed the Wright Company in 1909. This would later expand into the Curtiss-Wright company that was a dominant force in aircraft designs for years.

With the military seeing the advantages of airplanes on the battlefield, the aircraft and engine designs made great strides through the first World War, which is where this story really begins.

History of NACA

Just over 10 years after the Wright Brother's first flight, the U.S. Congress created the National Advisory Committee for Aeronautics (NACA) with the intent of coordinating aeronautical research already underway to support war-related projects. It was also meant to keep up with similar organizations in other countries. The act that formalized the creation of the NACA was approved March 3, 1915, and reads in part, "...It shall be the duty of the advisory committee for aeronautics to supervise and direct the scientific study of the problems of flight with a view to their practical solution." This was the research branch that studied aeronautics as a field of science in itself and thus a new field of science was born.

Source: NASA

1920 NACA Wind Tunnel

The NACA's Langley Memorial Aeronautical Laboratory's first wind tunnel construction was finished in 1920. Two years later, the NACA completed the variable-density tunnel. This was the advent of the use of Reynolds Numbers allowing the air density to be changed to scale the atmospheric pressure the same proportion as the airplane model is scaled. So, for example, a 1/20th scale model would use 20 times the atmospheric pressure to get the same aerodynamic affects. Aerodynamic forces, (lift, thrust, drag) could also be scaled.

Source: NASA

1922 NACA Wind Tunnel

In 1926, the Navy's Bureau of Aeronautics approached NACA to see if a circular cowling could be devised in such a way to reduce the drag of exposed radial engine cylinders without creating a cooling problem. A large, full-size "propeller" tunnel was built in 1927 to test this hypothesis. An airplane would be suspended on scales to measure thrust, drag, and lift in front of the tunnel that could produce different airspeeds impacting on the airplane.

1927 NACA Wind Tunnel

Following hundreds of tests, a NACA technical note by Fred E. Weick in November 1928 announced the Navy testing results which showed significant potential in increased speeds. At the same time, Langley acquired a Curtiss Hawk AT-5A biplane fighter from the Air Service and fitted a cowling around its blunt radial engine. The results were exhilarating. With little additional weight, the Hawk's speed jumped from 118 to 137 MPH, an increase of 16 percent.[1] (Remember that date, November of 1928, and see where cowlings appeared on the scene at Travel Air.) NACA produced standard airfoils that were used by airplane manufactures.

NACA would eventually transform into NASA and manage the US space programs.

Aircraft Boom in Wichita

Along with the introduction and widespread use of the gasoline engine in automobiles and airplanes came the oil boom. Jacob "Jake" Moellendick, a Kansas oil-field tycoon, envisioned a market for airplanes and thought Wichita—surrounded by vast tracts of undeveloped land with unobstructed vistas, but unsuitable for farming—was an ideal location to manufacture them. Reliability of airplanes was not great and the open plains offered lots of large fields as places to land in emergencies. There may have also been a misconception about the high winds of the plains being an advantage for aviation. The Wright Brothers selected Kill Devil Hills in North Carolina for testing their gliders because the hills were close to the glide slope, the sand made for softer landings and the winds were high (which they anticipated would keep the relative ground speed slow). In hindsight, they learned that the higher wind speeds also brought turbulence which made controlling the aircraft difficult.

Airplanes also offered oil field owners a much faster way to get to their far-flung drilling sites, so Jake had a personal interest in addition to the investment potential. He managed to attract Emil Matthew "Matty" Laird to come to Wichita in 1919 by offering him money and a place to manufacture. Matty had been designing and building biplanes in Chicago for eight years prior. His latest design was a three-place open-cockpit biplane called a Swallow.

The Swallow used a Curtiss OX-5 engine, popular as a lightweight engine for aircraft at that time. It had a decent power-to-weight ratio but wasn't very reliable. The advent of the radial engine, later on, would change that, but would also introduce a new problem: aerodynamic drag generated by all those cylinders sticking out into the airstream.

Laird Aviation Co. was founded in 1920 by Emil Laird from the purchase of the 6-month-old Wichita Aircraft Company and the factory of Watkins Aircraft Company. The Swallow flew well and Laird began preparing to commence production. Within weeks of the news about the Swallow had spread through the Midwest. This was the first successful commercial airplane manufactured in the United States.

By 1920 there was growing demand for a new commercial airplane. The World War I Curtiss airplanes were obsolete by the end of the war, and although there were small companies in the U.S. building new airplanes for commercial sale, the Swallow represented a significant value despite its high price of $6,500. Two of the employees hired to work for Laird Aviation were Lloyd Stearman and Walter Beech.

More than 40 Swallows were built and were well received. Although his airplanes were selling well, Matty's relationship with Jake was deteriorating. In October he sold the company rights to Jake and returned to Chicago where he quickly reestablished himself as a manufacturer of airplanes under the E.M. Laird Airplane Company. This is the company that built the Super Solution aircraft that won the 1931 Transcontinental race.

Jake then renamed the company in Wichita as the Swallow Airplane Company. Swallow produced a significant number of Swallow TPs, a training aircraft. A large proportion of pilots trained in the TP during the late 1920s and early '30s.

Source: Wichita State Univ. Libraries, Special Collections and University Archives
Lindbergh visiting Wichita in a Swallow

Creation of Travel Air

Lloyd Stearman, who had become chief engineer of Swallow, and co-worker Walter Beech recognized that aircraft design was changing. Wooden frames were becoming obsolete, giving way to steel-tube frames that offered more strength and greater longevity. However, Jake Moellendick, the president, was stubborn and rejected arguments from Lloyd Stearman, Walter Beech, and factory manager Bill Snook, that Swallows should follow the trend and build their frames from steel. Stearman and Beech (on their own time) built a steel-framed Swallow to demonstrate the idea to Jake, hoping it might win his approval. However, when it was shown to him, Jake exploded and told them to abandon their idea or the company. So they quit to start up their own company.

When Walter Beech and Lloyd Stearman left Swallow Aircraft, they persuaded fellow aviator Clyde Cessna to form Travel Air in 1925. They were able to convince Wichita investor Walter Innes Jr. to help them by investing in their venture. Travel Air was initially located in downtown Wichita on 471 W. 1st Street.

The building on 1st had previously been the home of Watkins Aircraft Company, builders of the Skylark. Watkins had been a blacksmith until an ember injured his eye. Unable to continue blacksmithing, he chose to try his hand as an entrepreneur in the aviation field. Watkins' prototype crashed killing the pilot, so he quit because he didn't want to be in a business where people would get killed.

Walter Innes Jr. was made the president and treasurer of Travel Air, Clyde Cessna was named vice president, and Walter Beech was the marketing and engineering test pilot. Olive Ann Mellor was hired as the 12th employee to be a bookkeeper, and soon to be the secretary who handled all correspondence, maintained records, and conducted transactions, eventually becoming office manager and then personal secretary to Walter.

Within a year, Walter Innes Jr. left the company. Clyde Cessna was then promoted to president, Walter Beech to vice president, and Lloyd Stearman treasurer. Travel Air quickly expanded and purchased the land on East Central in 1926.

Travel Air Model 5000

The Travel Air model 5000 was designed in 1926 and showed Cessna's influence with a single high-wing monoplane. This is the model aircraft that one aviator wanted the company to build a modified version of, however, Travel Air's backlog was too big all ready to commit to the pilot's short time frame, so Charles Lindbergh would have to find a different aircraft for his famous flight. Of course, as all historians know, he flew a Ryan built aircraft across the Atlantic. The Woolaroc Model 5000 airplane was the second aircraft to complete a trans-Pacific flight to Hawaii, and the first civilian aircraft to do so.

Note, the Model 5000 had the higher-reliability radial engine that made long flights over water possible.

Stearman left Travel Air in 1926 to form the Stearman Aircraft Company that was later purchased by Boeing Aircraft. Clyde Cessna followed the next year. Clyde wanted Travel Air to pursue a fully cantilevered wing (with no struts). Unable to convince Walter, but encouraged to follow his idea, Clyde sold his shares of the company and left to start up his own company. There wasn't any animosity between Clyde and Walter. Rather, they each just chose to follow their own path and design interests. Both Boeing and Cessna companies were very successful and are still going strong today.

Source: Vintage Air Photos

Woolaroc Model 5000

With the enactment of the Air Commerce Act in 1926, regulations now required the licensing of pilots and mechanics and the registration of aircraft. The law also required that aircraft comply with minimum airworthiness standards and receive certification by the Federal government. This added financial and regulatory pressure to the new industry and many airplane companies folded as a result. However, with Lindbergh's flight across the

Atlantic in 1927, the industry was re-invigorated. Airplanes were beginning to be seen in the public eye as a reliable form of transportation instead of mere barnstorming death machines. Companies that survived the introduction of regulations began to thrive.

In late 1927, Jake Moellendick bet most of the Swallow company fortune on a record-setting aircraft — the Dallas Spirit — which was lost on an attempt to set a new record flying to Asia concurrent with the Dole Air Race. The Swallow Airplane Company went into foreclosure in 1932.

Ted Wells Early Years

Source: James Rix

Young Ted Wells

Theodore (Ted) Arthur Wells was born March 12, 1907, in Corning, Iowa, but he was raised in Omaha, Nebraska. This was just four years after the Wright Brother's famous first flight and from the beginning, Ted was enamored with airplanes and built models of them as a child.

It so happened that the Bellanca Aircraft Company was located nearby in Omaha. He visited the factory every day on his way home from high school.[2] So inspired, when he was 15, he built an airplane in his family garage.[3] It was a single place cantilever monoplane powered by a 45-horsepower engine. It was apparently a sore subject in the family. "I got sent off to prep school and it sort of disappeared when I returned. They didn't think much of the idea."

One could only conjecture about its airworthiness. Ted thought that it would have been airworthy had it been completed. This was before any regulatory authority or rules existed though, so if you had the guts to try and take it to the air, then there wasn't anything preventing you from trying—except in this case, perhaps your parents.

Ted decided to further his education in the potentially promising field of air flight by attending the prestigious Princeton University. The Princeton School of Engineering had been founded in 1921, just a few years prior, with programs in Chemical, Geological, and Mechanical Engineering. It started with fewer than 100 students.[4]

Ted's first plane

Mechanical Engineering classes were held in the old
School of Science with a makeshift laboratory in a boiler
house. Ted specifically wanted a degree in Aeronautical
Engineering and was able to convince the school to allow
him to pursue it. In a reversal of traditional roles, Ted had
to tell the school what requirements he needed to satisfy
for a degree in Aeronautical Engineering.

There were only a couple books at the time on
aerodynamics and the national research branch NACA
had just constructed their first wind tunnel for measuring
aerodynamic forces. It was essentially a self-study
program where Ted reported to the dean once a week on
his progress. The dean was reading the same book, so he
could periodically ask Ted questions to validate that he
really was studying the material. There were no tests.

While a sophomore at Princeton University, Ted and a
fellow classmate got a chance to buy an old World War I
Jenny for $600. Thousands of surplus Jenny's were sold on

the civilian market after World War I, some for as little as $50, essentially flooding the market. Neither Ted nor his classmate had a pilot's license, so they came up with a scheme to buy it and rent it for rides and flying lessons to pay for it and fund their own flying lessons. (Both of their parents had previously refused to pay for flying lessons.)

As part of their scheme to acquire the Jenny, the twosome learned that Princeton had a policy they could use to their advantage: students whose parents had difficulty raising tuition could postpone payment until the end of the semester. So, Ted and his friend informed the school that their parents were struggling financially and used the tuition money their parents had given them to buy the plane.

Source: State Archives NSW

Curtiss JN-4 (Jenny)

Ted and his friend, now in business, would offer their plane for lessons and rides, charging $25 per hour. By paying a flight instructor $10 of that, and keeping $15 profit to pay off the airplane (and tuition!). Their customers were drawn from a "sucker list" of more prosperous and adventurous upperclassmen that they also used for bumming rides to the airfield.[5]

During Spring break, Ted found himself abandoned at the Hadley airfield more than 20 miles away from the university with no money and no ride back to school. He waited until dusk, but no potential ride showed up. He was determined not to walk the distance back to campus. With only four hours and twenty minutes of flying instruction, he decided it was time to solo without an endorsement from the instructor. He cranked up the plane, flew to Princeton and landed in a field frequently used by barnstormers.

According to Ted, "The Dean got excited because Princeton sophomores were not supposed to have motor vehicles." Fortunately, that stunt did not get him kicked out. This incident, however, was apparently picked up by the New York Times as a box story on the front page. This is how Ted's father learned that he had purchased the Jenny. Ted said his parents did not force him to sell the airplane. "They were resigned to the fact that if I was going to be in the airplane business, I should learn to fly. But they didn't exactly like the way I was doing it."[6] By the end of the semester, they had not raised enough to pay for tuition, so they were forced to sell the Jenny for the $600 they paid for it in order to pay the college.

Over the summer of 1927, Ted purchased a Travel Air Model B and was barnstorming in Kansas and Nebraska offering $1.00 rides at county fairs. It's not clear where he got the money to purchase this airplane. The Travel Air B, later called the Model 2000, was designed to use the Curtiss OX-5 engine.

Source: San Diego Air and Space Museum Archives

Travel Air Model B

After he got his pilot's license, Ted used the plane for "social purposes" in his words eluding to a method for picking up girls. On one trip, he landed in a hay field near Boston as there weren't runways to speak of at that time. Upon landing, he broke an axle. He managed to find the Travel Air distributor in Boston and got the spare axle replaced and returned to Princeton. Sometime later, the

Dean called Ted into his office and asked Ted "what is this about," showing him a bill to the university from a hay farmer with the article from the New York Times attached. Apparently, the farmer was claiming Ted damaged his hay by landing in his field and wanted compensation. The Dean and Ted decided on an amount Ted should pay to settle with the farmer and they never heard from him again so it was an equitable amount.

Source: James Rix

Curtiss OX-5 engine

During the summers of 1928 and 1929, Ted worked as an engineering apprentice at the Travel Air Company. He arranged to buy a Model 4000 Travel Air with a 200 HP Wright radial engine in July of 1928. Before Ted picked it up, the airplane was being used to test a new set of wings with a lower-drag Navy N-9 airfoil section that increased the speed from 130 mph to 150 mph. Ted convinced Walter to keep the wings on the airplane as he was confident that he would be successful racing with it. With the new wings, it was designated as a Model D4000. He also had Walter mount the wing fittings internally to further reduce drag.

Photo: Jerry Impellezerri

Ted with his D4000 Travel Air

That summer and fall, Ted won many races in the Midwest. Ted made additional modifications to the airplane to decrease drag and increase the speed including narrower landing gear wheels and a cowling around the engine (not shown in the picture). Unfortunately, the airplane got destroyed in a hangar fire in the fall of 1929 after it won a succession of air races.

Ted joined Travel Air part-time in 1928 as a demonstration pilot during the summer of his junior year at Princeton. Ted then was hired by Travel Air full-time as a design engineer after he graduated in 1929 and filling the engineering void left by Cessna and Stearman.

Model R

Herbert Rawdon, and his assistant Walter E. Burnham began working on their own to design the Model R, which Beech accepted and built, just in time to enter the 1929 race on September the 2nd. Construction started on Model R just ten weeks before 1929 National Air Races. While Ted was not directly involved with this project; it should be noted that the exposure to Rawdon's talent along with his formal education in aeronautical engineering gave him the tools for designing great aircraft. Drag reducing features such as NACA engine cowlings and wheel pants were new concepts that were on the leading edge of aerodynamic technology of the day. This was a new field of engineering that Ted was active in. Recall that the NACA engine cowling test report was completed for the Navy only a few months before this and Ted had already put a cowling on his model D4000.

Image: Western Reserve Historical Society, Cleveland, Ohio

1929 Air Race flyer

The biggest event of the 1929 National Air Races was the "unlimited free-for-all race," on September 2, 1929. There were 11 entrants in the race, but the expected contest was between the Army's Curtiss P-3-A powered by a Wasp engine and the US Navy's Curtiss F6C-C Hawk, powered by a D-12. Both of these planes were frontline pursuit ships, the fastest airplanes the military had to offer and this was the first time since 1925 that the two services flew against each other. The first of the five production Army P-3 aircraft later became a second XP-3A and was used in the development of the NACA Cowling. Also racing was a Lockheed Vega, and the Travel Air Model R "Mystery Ship" being piloted by Doug Davis, a Travel Air dealer and air racer.[7]

Source: U.S. Air Force

Army's 1929 Air Race entry

It was dubbed the "Mystery Ship" because it was built in secrecy away from Travel Air production. When it arrived in Cleveland, it was immediately moved to a hangar and covered with a tarpaulin. During the race, the Mystery

Ship took the early lead but had to re-circle a pylon that was cut short on the second lap—the rules required missed pylons to be re-circled. As he was taking the tight turn, he momentarily blacked out and wasn't sure he had re-circled the pylon, so he ended up circling it again. This caused Davis to be passed by the other planes, but despite the penalty and extra pylon rounding, he was able to take the lead again and win with an average speed of 194.9 mph and clocking 235 mph in the straight-a-ways. The Army Curtiss P-3 came in second in the free-for-all race with an average speed of 186 mph.

Source: San Diego Air and Space Museum

Navy's 1929 Air Race entry

The Model R was faster than any other civilian airplane had ever flown before. News reporters jumped all over the military and peppered them with questions of how could a civilian airplane beat the fastest US military airplanes. Of course, the reasons were not simple, but it was still an embarrassment for the military.

Travel Air Model R "Mystery Ship"

The defeat of the military shocked the country resulting in the total abandonment of the biplane in the Army and a few years later in the Navy. To illustrate the significance of the defeat, it may be worth noting that the Aircraft Year Book of 1929 details the National Air Races of 1928. This was also the last time the Army took part in a race against civilian aircraft.

Note in this picture of the Navy's 1931 race entry how the Navy returned with a full engine cowling, streamlined wing struts, wheel pants, and without the lower wing. The Mystery Ship didn't participate in this race. Even this configuration with the high wing would cause the airplane to want to pitch up at higher speeds from the wing drag well above the center of thrust requiring considerable control/trim downforce and associated drag.

Source: US Navy National Museum of Naval Aviation

Navy's 1931 Race entry

As part of the National Air Races, Ted flew his D4000 Travel Air in the 1929 Portland Derby. This was a cross-country race from Portland to Cleveland which involved navigation skills as well as aircraft speed. Ted won this race receiving a whopping $10,000 in prize money. Ted also loaned his airplane to Louise Thaden who used it to win the National Women's Air Derby as well.

1929 was the same year he graduated from Princeton and the Aviation giant Curtiss-Wright bought Travel Air.

The next transcontinental race was held in 1931 and was won by none other than the now famous Jimmy Doolittle in a Laird Super Solution. He was initially planning on flying a Mystery S, but during a speed-trial prior to the race, it lost its ailerons and a piece of the right wing. Jimmy parachuted to safety but the aircraft was lost. It was a case of aileron flutter.

Ted's 1929 National Air Derby Trophy

Aerodynamic forces cause the control surface to begin to flap in the airstream. This flapping motion happens suddenly and creates enough loads on the control surface that it frequently fails structurally and departs the aircraft, sometimes, as this case, taking a chunk of the wing with it.

This was not a new problem as World War 1 aircraft were plagued with aileron flutter. Both NACA and The Royal Aeronautical Establishment created Flutter Subcommittees just to address this issue. Now known as *aeroelasticity*, it is a dynamic instability of an elastic structure in a fluid flow where a lack of dampening will result in an increasing self-oscillation and aerodynamic loading. The problem at the time was somewhat solved as a trial and error method by stiffening the wings which worked at slower speeds. But, as aircraft speeds were increasing the problem would continue to re-emerge.

The highly competitive attempts to break speed records and to capture coveted air-race prizes pushed designers to ever-higher speeds in which flutter encounters, usually catastrophic, occurred during high-speed runs. Racers would stiffen their wings with plywood veneer in order to avoid flutter. This prompted Bill Stout, the all-metal Ford Trimotor builder, to tout his airplane was "free of Veneer-eal disease." [8]

In some cases, flutter would occur without catastrophic failure and the pilot would be able to slow down and land without crashing. Having an opportunity to improvise a design fix, the racer would sometimes come up with creative ways to address the problem. Leon Tolve describes such an incident from the 1934 National Races: "Racers kept encountering wing-tip flutter. Each time the wingspan was reduced by cutting off part of the wing tip until the flutter stopped. As a result, the wing area was finally reduced from its original value of 78 ft. 2" down to 42 ft. 2", and the pilot ended with flutter-free airplane!"[9]

Ted's first task as a design engineer at Travel Air was to design the wing of the Model 6000. His role as an apprentice was short lived as he rapidly took on more design work. Both Walter and Ted got married in 1930. Walter married Olive Ann Mellor and Ted married

Margery Adair. Marge was a warm, considerate lady from Omaha who also happened to be a Firestone heiress.

Ted and Marge Wells

Model 16

The Curtiss-Wright CW-12 Sport Trainer and CW-16 Light Sport (also marketed under the Travel Air brand that Curtiss-Wright had recently acquired) were high-performance training aircraft designed by Ted Wells and Herbert Rawdon in the early 1930s.

The CW-12 and CW-16 shared the same basic design as conventional single-bay biplanes with the upper wing braced with N-struts. The pilot and instructor sat in tandem, open cockpits, the forward cockpit of the CW-12 having a single seat, while the CW-16's forward cockpit could seat two passengers side-by-side. Both versions of the aircraft were available in a variety of engine choices, and some CW-16s were exported as trainers to the air forces of Bolivia and Ecuador.[10]

Photo: Tim Vickers

Model 16 Travel Air

Model W4B

In his spare time in 1930, Ted designed and built the racing biplane Model W4B, also known as a Wells Special. It had the same one-piece inter-wing struts later seen on the Model 17 and all-internal wing fittings. He used the engine from his D4000 that got destroyed in the hanger fire. Apparently, the engine survived the fire. The Wells Special was built in the experimental department of Travel Air and had the same tail number (N6128) as his Model D4000. Unfortunately, during one of the test flights, he was flying at 200 mph only five-hundred feet off the ground when both ailerons tore off the wings. Again control surface flutter was the culprit that caused this crash. Ted managed to bail out and pull his parachute just in time. He landed in

the mud suffering only a broken ankle. That event made
him an honorary member of the Caterpillar Club, a title
given to those that have parachuted out of airplanes.
Control surface flutter at higher airspeeds would continue
to plague Travel Air as the root cause was unknown at the
time. This was one of Ted's challenges to try to solve.

Model W4B – Wells Special

In 1931, while still in Wichita, Ted began producing the
next design for Travel Air. The model 17 was a four-place
enclosed-cockpit biplane with an unconventional
placement of the top wing aft of the bottom wing. This was
done to improve upon the visibility associated with the
wing standard configuration.

Curtiss-Wright moved Travel Air to St. Louis in 1931 to
consolidate the company in a declining economy where
Ted served as chief engineer. Herbert Rawdon elected to
stay in Wichita. He later became a draftsman for Lockheed
in 1933, then Boeing. In 1940, he returned to work for

Beech Aircraft as chief engineer under Ted Wells, who was still serving as Vice President of Engineering.

By the early 30s, the economy was in decline and the engineering department at Travel Air was reduced to three people including Ted. One of the other three was Kendall Perkins who went on to become engineering vice president of McDonnell Aircraft and helped build the Mercury Capsule that put the first astronauts into space.

Since Ted already had a pilot's license, they decided they didn't need a test pilot so they gave Ted that responsibility as well and let test pilot Charles Dolson go. Dolson eventually went on to become the president and then CEO and Chairman of the Board of Delta Airlines. Curtiss-Wright then sent Ted to Omaha to get a mechanic's license in addition to his pilot's license. According to Ted, "The thinking was that if you flew across the country to get to the school, then you were automatically qualified to get the license." That's a testimony of how unreliable airplanes were back then. Cross-country trips often led to mechanical failures along the way which is also what made the plains a good place for an aircraft manufacturer.

Walter Beech was very impressed with Ted's Model 17 "staggerwing" drawings and presented them to Curtiss-Wright management to persuade them to build it. Curtiss-Wright directors declined to pursue the program for financial reasons. The economy had taken a nose dive as the country was now deep in the Depression. About a fifth of all banks were closed, unemployment had reached 25%, and country-wide corporate profits were down 90%. This was the peak of the Depression era, but they didn't know that. So, they reasoned that if there wasn't any demand for the smaller, less-expensive aircraft, there wouldn't be any for a larger four-place plane that would be more expensive.

Desiring to continue Ted's Model 17 design, Walter Beech, Olive Ann Beech, K.K. Shaul, and Ted Wells resigned from Curtiss-Wright's Aircraft division to start up a new company to produce the Model 17. They likely attracted others in joining them to return to Wichita and picked up some past Travel Air employees that elected to stay in Wichita during the move to St. Louis. Given the economic situation, this appears to have been highly speculative at best—if not downright insane.

Beech Aircraft

Walter Beech, Olive Ann Beech, Ted Wells, K.K. Shaul, and C.G. Yankey become the principle founders of Beech Aircraft Company in April 1932. Walter was named President and Ted Wells was named Vice President of Engineering and Chief Designer. C.G. Yankey was a friend of the Beech's and a prime investor, so he was named Vice President. He later became the owner of Mooney Aircraft. K. K. Shaul, general manager at Travel Air and comptroller before relocating to St. Louis, was named Treasurer. Olive Ann was named Secretary.

Source: James Rix

Ted Wells, V.P., Beech Aircraft Company

The newly formed Beech Aircraft Company picked up other employees wanting to return to Wichita as well as some that had previously left Travel Air to remain in Wichita when it moved to Saint Louis. Travel Air went out of business that same year due in part to the departure of key management and engineering staff. Walter Beech with K. K. Shaul and Ted Wells initially leased part of the Cessna facility which is now known as the Pawnee Plant.[11] The first four aircraft were produced there before they procured the old Travel Air Building on East Central.

Model 17

Ted's design of the Model 17 was intended to be a business airplane that could carry four people in comfort. It was also designed to be fast. He used the same Navy airfoil section that was used on his W4B racing aircraft to minimize drag. It also incorporated many other drag-reduction methods he learned in aeronautical engineering and with the design of the Mystery S. This included engine cowling, wheel pants, streamlined wing struts and even the guy wires were streamlined. The main landing-gear wheels could actually retract inside the wheels pants with a hand crank to further reduce drag. Placing the top wing aft of the bottom wing was done for visibility, but in hindsight, he found it also promoted the bottom wing to stall first causing the plane to pitch forward and regain lift without the top wing losing lift.

The result was an incredibly fast and stable airplane. This production airplane was also faster than most military planes and successfully competed in many air races. A couple were built with an even larger 700 HP engines. The nose length of the airplane would vary depending on the weight of the engine. Since the large engine weighed considerably more, the proper center of gravity was maintained by shortening the engine mount distance from the firewall. This provided an easy method for utilizing several engines with different weights in the evolution of the Model 17.

During 1933, Ted Wells and his design staff reworked the original design to make it less expensive and more marketable. They changed to a smaller engine, a much lighter airframe, and a major innovation for the private pilot, fully retractable landing gear. This was the first commercial aircraft to have retractable gear. Doing this also solved a problem with the previous gear being too close together, which gave the aircraft a bad tendency to do ground loops on landings, especially in crosswinds. This was another hindsight benefit of having the staggered wing as it could retract into the lower wing. Traditionally placed lower wings would have been too far aft to provide the space needed to stow the gear.

Source: Kansas Aviation Museum

Model 17

He also increased the air flowing through the engine compartment by adding exit ducts. This increased the amount cooling air flow for the cylinders finding a good balance between low drag and sufficient engine cooling.

In 1933, Ted hired Clyde Cessna's nephew, Wayne Wallace, who had graduated as an aeronautical engineer but was struggling to find a job. His first job was to do stress analysis. This was a weakness of Ted's as he had difficulties with the Aeronautics Branch of the Department of Commerce, forerunner of the FAA, in the certification effort because of a failure to perform adequate load analysis.

The redesigned Model 17 listed in 1934 for $8,000 instead of $12,000 for the 200 mph fixed gear 17R Model. The new design was called the Model B17L and carried serial #3. It was completed in early 1934 and became the first real production aircraft for the 2-year-old company. On February 2, 1934, it made its first flight, marking the beginning of a successful year for Beech in which 19 aircraft were built.[12]

This was enough for the company to purchase the old Travel Air factory and airfield which had remained abandoned since Travel Air was relocated to Saint Louis. Sales increased yet again in 1935 to 30 airplanes.

Note the instrument panel doesn't have the standard basic T instruments arrangements of flight instruments that are used today, let alone any attitude indicator. The Model 17 predated Instrument Flight Rules (IFR). Flying at night was considered dangerous and only performed by stunt pilots. As such, there are also no instrument lights. The prominent instrument was a turn and bank which was used for coordinating turns. On close examination, you can see a strap to hold the window knob. The window mechanism was taken from an Oldsmobile. It is suspected that without that strap, it had a tendency to work its way open from engine vibrations.

Original Instrument Panel

Another item to note is how the instruments are mounted to a panel protruding from the panel behind. This is a shock mounted instrument panel to reduce instrument needles from bouncing with engine vibrations. This is the first aircraft where this is done and carried over into the King Airs. The throw over yoke is one of Ted's innovations and a Beech trademark later to be used on the Bonanza. You can also clearly see the prominent Beech 'B' logo on the yoke. This symbol would become synonymous with quality.

Several versions of the Model 17 were produced. Most notable was the longer tail in the D Model for improved stability.

Source: Kansas Aviation Museum

Model A17FL

With lots of testing, and analysis performed by many organizations including NACA, a better understanding of flutter was achieved. With the addition of a balancing weight in front of the pivot point of the control surfaces, the problem was addressed for the airplane speeds that were achieved by the Model 17.

Suffix	Engine	Cylinders	HP
A	Wright R-760-E2	7	350
B	Jacobs L-5 (R-830-1)	7	285
D	Jacobs L-6 (R-915A3)	7	330
E	Wright R-760-E1	7	285
F	Wright R-1820-F11	9	690
FS	Wright SR-1820-F3 (supercharged)	9	710
L	Jacobs L-4 (R-755D)	7	225
R	Wright R-975-E2 or E3	9	420-450
S	P&W R-985-AN-1 or AN-3	9	450

Source: Wikipedia

Different Model 17 upgrades

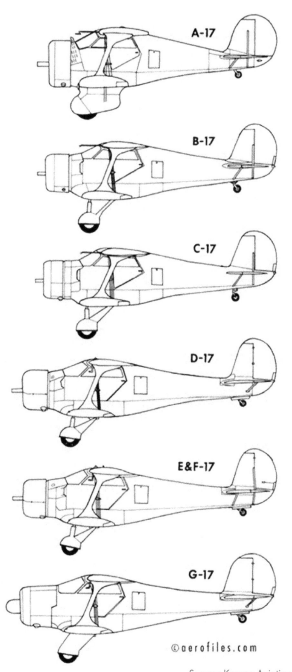

Source: Kansas Aviation Museum

Different Model 17 upgrades

Production of the model 17 finally ended in 1948 primarily due to manufacturing costs generated by the large amount of time spent handcrafting. A total of 785 Staggerwings were built including 105 that went to the Air Force and 320 to the Navy.

Staggerwings are still beloved by their owners and are popular models for restorations. 282 airframes are in existence today, either in flying condition, need of maintenance or restoration. The history, status, and photos of most serial numbers can be found on http://beech17.net.

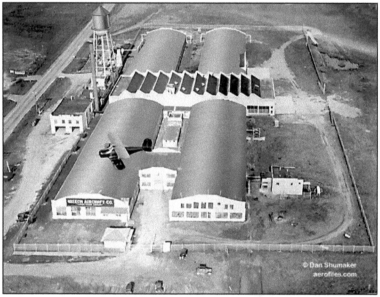

Source: Aerofiles

Early Beech Aircraft Plant

Once production numbers increased, so did the capacity of the factory. The original Travel Air building (in the lower left in the picture) was duplicated three more times as interconnecting buildings. An administration building was also built to the north of the manufacturing buildings.

Model 18

The next creation of Ted's began at the end of 1934. The Beech Model 18 was the introduction of the first business aircraft to the market. The Department of Commerce put out a specification for what it considered to be an aircraft there was a demand for in the general market. The department wasn't planning on buying airplanes though. Knowing that the labor cost involved in the fabrication of the Model 17, Walter and Ted saw this as an opportunity to transition over to the more popular metal airframe and dramatically reduce manufacture time.

Ted's design was fairly conventional for the time, including twin radial engines, all-metal semi-monocoque construction with fabric-covered control surfaces and a tail-wheel undercarriage. Less conventional was the twin tailfin configuration. It was designed to be as small as possible within the Department of Commerce specifications. The Lockheed Electra, also built to this specification, was larger and heavier and thus didn't perform as well. This gave the marketing advantage to Beech.

Since the use of aluminum alloys for structural parts of aircraft was a new application, replacing steel and wood construction, there was very little information published on the metallurgy and processing of aluminum alloys. To

45

fill this void, Ted authored a textbook on entitled Wells'
Manual of Aircraft Materials and Manufacturing
Processes.[13] He then taught a course with this book
through the University of Kansas extension department.

Model 18

In 1955, deliveries of the Model E18S began. The E18S
featured a fuselage that was extended 6-inches higher for
more headroom in the passenger cabin. All later Beech 18s
(sometimes called Super 18s) featured this taller fuselage,
and some earlier models (including one AT-11) were
modified with this larger fuselage. The Model H18,
introduced in 1963, featured an optional tricycle undercarriage. The undercarriage was actually developed for
earlier model aircraft under a Supplemental Type
Certificate (STC) by Volpar, and installed in H18s at the
factory during manufacture.

The military first took interest in the Model 18 as they
wanted a twin-tail airplane to test flutter on the B-24 (also
a twin tail). It so happened that a Model 18 airplane was

readily available for testing. This led to the first military contract for the AT-7 that was used by the Army Air Force as a navigation trainer and featured an acrylic dome for celestial navigation.

Eventually, 32 versions of the Model 18, also known as the Model C-45, were built and used by the United States government as a navigation training and transport aircraft. Military versions included personnel transport, photo reconnaissance, and trainers for bombardiers. The highly adaptable design also became a mail plane, a utility aircraft, and a distance- and speed-record breaker.

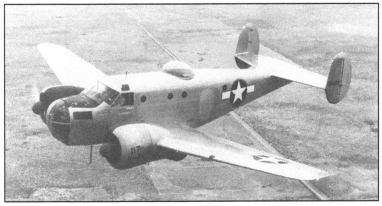

Source: US Air Force

AT-11 in flight

The success of the Beech 18 ensured the success of Beech Aircraft Corporation throughout the 1940s. Beech introduced the D-18S Model in October 1945, with structural modifications for increased payload and new engines and landing gear. Tail number N522B was used as an air ambulance for 15 years, flying over a million miles and transporting nearly fifteen thousand patients. The AT-

11 was developed as a bombing trainer during the war. They would practice dropping dummy bombs on target ships created on the desert floor.[14]

A total of 109 H18s were built with tricycle undercarriage, and another 240 earlier-model aircraft were modified with this. Construction of the Beechcraft Model 18 ended in 1970 with a final Model H18 going to Japan Airlines. A total of 8,980 Model 18s and variants were built.

Source: Beech Log - April 16, 1943

Dropping dummy bombs on the desert floor

XA-38

The US Army Air Forces contracted with Beech Aircraft in 1942 to build two prototypes of a Model 28 "Destroyer," a.k.a. "Grizzly," a heavy attack aircraft designed to fulfill a requirement to replace the Douglas A-20s that were currently in service. By this time, Ted had built a formidable engineering team that tackled the task of designing it with abandon. The Beech Model XA-38 was designed to accommodate a 75mm cannon in the nose and six 50-caliber machine guns, two in the lower fuselage nose, two in a turret on the dorsal, and two in a turret on the ventral. It could also carry up to 2,000 lbs. of external stores.

Source: U.S. Air Force

XA-38 in flight

The flight testing performance for the Model XA-38 was phenomenal. Its speed (376 mph) was comparable to the faster single-engine fighters. The P-51 chase plane couldn't keep up at lower altitudes.

Had it gone into production, the Model A-38 (Experimental 'X' dropped) would have been the forerunner to today's A-10 Warthog. The 30mm Gatling gun on the A-10 tank buster is small compared to the

75mm cannon that was mounted on the XA-38. In fact, the T15E1 (M10) cannon was specifically designed for the A-38. This cannon, with an 84-inch barrel, could fire a 15-pound shell every two seconds. With a speed of over 2000-feet per second, these shells could go through almost four inches of steel armor. This was more than a tank buster: it was a battleship destroyer. The gun was successfully test fired from the aircraft in flight proving its feasibility.

Photo: Tom Fey

75mm Cannon for A-38

As it turned out, the A-38 used the same engines as the Boeing B-29 heavy bomber which had priority over it and all the engines went to Boeing. Also, the A-26 was getting all the 50-caliber machine guns, so dummy turrets were put on the prototypes. No production contract was awarded after the two XA-38 prototypes were built since the war was winding down. Nonetheless, the Model-38 leaves us a true "what if" question: What impact would it would have made in the war had it gone into production?

A-26 Wings

In 1943, Ted went to Douglas Aircraft to see if Beech Aircraft could do some of the work for the A-26 Invader attack bomber program. He was successful and Beech contracted with Douglas Aircraft to design and build the wings for the A-26. There were many design and manufacturing challenges that needed to be worked out and Ted got directly involved.

Even as an executive, Ted continued to keep a hands-on approach to aircraft design and solving technical issues. Max Eaton, a manufacturing engineer recalls, "Mr. Wells became daily involved solving these detail problems and he was quite capable in this area. I also was impressed with his technique of leadership. He would convene a meeting of all involved areas of the manufacturing, planning, scheduling, tooling, quality control and anyone else who might contribute to the problem. Ted would then simply state the problem under consideration for the meeting and ask for suggestions and/or comments from those present. He would then sit back and listen to anyone and everything that was a suggestion, comment, or complaint for about 30 minutes. Ted would then say, 'After listening to you gentlemen, I believe you have come to a consensus which is…' " [15]

Bonanza

Photo: Bill Larkins

V-35 Bonanza

Walter Beech anticipated the end of the war and Ted oversaw the design of a single-engine, 4-seat Bonanza with a "V" tail with Ralph Harmon as the project engineer. All the design work was done with unpaid overtime. The industry was struggling as military contracts were gone and the commercial market hadn't emerged yet. In order to keep the airplane small, Ted specified that it be a 2 7/8 (slightly less than three seats) place airplane knowing that the design would grow into the four-place airplane as the natural part of what's referred to as design creep meaning that project developments have a tendency to expand past their initial concept. The first aircraft crashed due to the elusive flutter problem, this time with the tail itself.

The V-tail concept was invented and patented in 1930 by Polish engineer Jerzy Rudlicki. Due to two tail surfaces instead of the standard three, it significantly reduced drag. With its retractable landing gear, lightweight aluminum-shell construction, and its distinctive "V" tail, the legendary Bonanza was, by far, the fastest and most efficient of all affordable, full-sized light planes on the market.[16] The Bonanza was much smaller and with lower horsepower, but it carried the same number of people the same distance in the same amount of time for about a third the cost. This airplane dominated business and executive aviation at a time when many other plane makers were going out of business.

After Travel Air relocated to the E. Central location, Knoll Airplane Company, another upstart aircraft company, temporarily set up in the former Travel Air's downtown location. They purchased machines and tooling from Swallow's bankruptcy. They then built a new facility on the corner of Kellogg and Webb. At the time, it was the biggest manufacturing facility in Wichita. It closed in Oct 1929 and the property was sold to short-lived Yellow Air Cab Company, then Straughn Aircraft. This facility was then purchased by Beech Aircraft in 1940 to become Plant 2, the manufacturing facility for the Bonanza.

The V-tail design was stopped in 1982 and replaced by a conventional tail because it was susceptible to structural failure at high speeds. This was not an issue as long as it was operated within its published airspeed limitations; the speeds it was certified for. However, it was unofficially nicknamed "Doctor Killer" as the ease at which it could be flown past the maximum allowable airspeed made it dangerous for pilots, at least for those who would push it beyond its published airspeed limitations thinking there was lots of design margin. Regretfully, there were no warnings leading to catastrophic failure. Once a pilot pushed the speed to the point of structural failure, it was too late to do anything about it.

Over 17,000 Bonanzas of a variety of models have been built, making it one of the most produced aircraft in the world and the plane in continuous production for the longest of any airplane in history.

T-34

The Bonanza would morph into a series of other successful airplanes. The T-34 Mentor, a modified Bonanza, would become America's (and the world's) preferred military-pilot trainer for a decade. The contract for this trainer was awarded by Navy competition between Beech and Fairchild. Beech designed the T-34 using much of the Bonanza design. Fairchild initially won the contract because the Beech T-34 wasn't designed according to the military handbook. For example, Beech opted to save cost and weight by using a radio that only had a few frequencies instead of a very expensive and heavy radio with over a thousand frequencies as specified. Beech rationalized that a trainer didn't need the full gamut of frequencies for fulfilling its training mission. Although the contract was awarded to Fairchild, it was discovered that their entry couldn't meet the minimum required airspeed due to its heavier weight. The following week, the contract with Fairchild was pulled and a contract with Beech was made. This trainer was replaced after a very successful life by another Beech Model, the T-6 Texan II in 1990, which as of 2018 is still used to train all US military aviators.

Photo: Bill Larkins

Model T-34

Model 34 "Twin-Quad"

The high-wing V-tailed Model 34, a logical familial follow-on to the already successful Model 33 Bonanza, began development in 1943 and first flew in October 1947. Projected to have a maximum speed of 300 mph, the "Twin-Quad" was only able to achieve 230 mph on early flights. It had a design gross weight of 20,000 lbs. and could carry 20 passengers.[17]

The Model 34 took to the air for the first time on October 1, 1947, with Beech Chief Pilot Vern L. Carstens at the controls. The first flight was uneventful and the initial report from the test pilot was, "We have another outstanding Beechcraft!"[18]

Photo: Johan Visschedijk

Model 34 on ground

The Model 34 "Twin-Quad" was designed for feeder airlines. Beech's solution had two propellers ("Twin") were driven through individual clutches by four engines ("Quad") buried in its wings. The geared, supercharged Lycoming eight-cylinder engines each produced 400 hp. at 3,300 rpm. With each pair of engines interconnected, engine-out problems would be less severe, and flight testing showed that the airplane could climb to 19,000 ft. with one engine shut down.

The only prototype spent nearly 200 hours in flight test until a January 1948 crash resulted in the death of the co-pilot and injury to the pilot and two observers.[19] An electrical fire started so the pilot called for the co-pilot to shut down the electrical system. He inadvertently hit the crash bar which killed all the engines instead. The co-pilot didn't respond when the pilot ordered the engines restarted so the pilot restarted the engines. When the pilot looked up, they were aimed at a farmhouse. He took

evasive action which missed the house but was too low
and the wing struck the ground.[20]

Source: San Diego Air and Space Museum Archive

Model 34 in flight

The investment of time and expense required to build
another prototype, along with a vanishing market
convinced the company to drop the project, but not before
spending a total of $6-million in development. Operators
bought up surplus C-47s, Lockheeds, and used Beech
Model 18s at a fraction of the cost of a new aircraft.

The Model 50 Twin Bonanza

Other spin-offs of the Bonanza evolved as markets opened
up. The Twin Bonanza wasn't just a Bonanza with twin
engines because the fuselage was also widened and
lengthened. This was a rapidly developed airplane that
was designed and flown in 1949. It was certified and
started production in 1951. This was adapted to the L-23
for the US Army. During a demonstration flight full of

soldiers, the plane crashed while trying to land over a tree line. Fortunately, everyone on board walked away which made the Army impressed with the structural integrity.

Variants Models 55, 56, & 58 Baron, Model 95 Travel Air

Beech Aircraft continues to produce aircraft which were either inspired by Ted Wells or utilize parts of the designs that were developed under his guidance. After over half a century, the Bonanza (with a straight tail and six seats) is still manufactured today— the longest continuously-built airplane design in the world. Elements of the Bonanza would find themselves on the Twin Bonanza, Queen Air, and King Air aircraft as well. The wing loft and structure outboard of the engine nacelle of the King Air were taken from the Bonanza wing design. The Model 1900 19 passenger commuter also used the same wing design except that its main spar was one piece that passed through the fuselage.

Beech airplanes were considered the Cadillac of aircraft due to the quality design and reliability compared with other aircraft. Beech Aircraft (later known as Beechcraft) was also a preferred place to work due to the family type environment along with good pay. Demand for employment at Beech was high and those that were hired felt they were set for life. Traditions included employee days at Joyland, the local amusement park, and firework shows at the Beech lakes. The company newsletter, the Beech Log had articles from every department that included what their employees were doing outside of Beech. This included how they did in their bowling leagues, where they went on vacation, and in the case of Ted and other Beechcrafters that raced Snipes, how they placed in sailing regattas.

Sailing

Source: James Rix

Race at Santa Fe Lake

One Sunday afternoon in 1938, after their move to Wichita with the startup of Beech, Ted and Marge Wells drove out to Santa Fe Lake to watch the boats. Ted was intrigued by the performance of a small dinghy called a Snipe. As they were leaving the lake, the couple stopped at a stand to buy a bottle of pop. Wells asked another bystander if any of the boats were for sale. He bought his first boat for $100.[21] It had bed sheets for sails.

It was then that Ted decided to race sailboats rather than airplanes as it was becoming difficult to find the time for racing airplanes. He joined the recently formed Wichita Sailing Club (WSC) at Santa Fe Lake, East of Wichita. To call Santa Fe a lake is a stretch. It is a 200-acre reservoir originally built by the Santa Fe Railroad as a water supply for its steam locomotives. The lake has completely evaporated on more than one occasion. I recall one occurrence that revealed an engine block some early club member had used as a mooring anchor.

Ted got proficient at racing on Santa Fe Lake in no time. He was instrumental in organizing the club's first invitational regatta and began trailering his boat (a 15 ½ foot Snipe) around the country to participate in other regattas. Ted raced on several boats before he purchased 6025 from Varalyay, a professional boat builder in California. These turned out to be fast boats. His regular crew was Art Lippitt, a metallurgist who also worked at Beech Aircraft. Ted never accredited his success racing sailboats to his knowledge of aeronautics.

"When I first started winning races with some consistency, everyone assumed that it was my experience with airplanes and my supposedly superior knowledge of aerodynamics that was my secret for success. I finally got tired of explaining that having a knowledge of theoretical aerodynamics was a hindrance if anything, and there wasn't any Arthur-Murray-in-a-Hurry method of learning how to win races."[22] Although Ted may not have used his knowledge of aerodynamics, he did use his problem-solving skills to approach sailboat racing and understood the importance of practice.

Ted & Marge on the dock

The Wichita Sailing Club regattas became popular and widely publicized events and had a large social element in addition to racing Snipes. Saturday evening dinners after the day's races were black-tie affairs that typically included ballroom dancing held in downtown Wichita.

There were many connections between Beech Aircraft and Snipe racing on Santa Fe Lake. The Beech Log, employee newsletter, often featured articles about employees including Ted participating in Snipe regattas. Other Beech personnel also followed suit and were also members of the Wichita Sailing Club including Engineering Vice Presidents Chet Rembleski and Linden Blue.

Pierre Havre reminisces about a regatta in Dallas: "By the final race of the Southwestern Championships, Ted Wells was leading. I'd raced against him in both 1945 and 1946 International Championships and knew that he was an outstanding Snipe sailor. We were opposites in almost every way. Ted was usually the oldest competitor and I the youngest. Ted was normally conservative, while I often took chances. Ted was Vice President and Head of Engineering for Beech Aircraft, and I was a high school student. Because of his job, he had more innovative gadgets than anyone in the Snipe class. I, on the other hand, purposefully sailed simpler and more sparsely equipped boats than my competitors. Despite our differences, we both won the majority of races that we entered. This taught me that there is usually more than one way to achieve the same goal."

"Of course, one way is usually accepted and popular, and the other isn't! And (no surprise here) most of my life, I've chosen the latter! So by the final race in this event, I was in second place behind Ted in the standings and the only sailor with any realistic chance of beating him. I needed to finish ahead of him with one additional boat between us, and I figured that Bob Carrick was certainly capable of beating Ted Wells."

"I had a comfortable lead until the next-to-last leg, when the fitting fastening my jib to the deck gave way. Luckily we were on the downwind leg, and were able to hold our lead around the final mark, but when we started back to windward, I knew many boats would pass us before the finish line. Ted rounded the last mark just behind us, and was soon able to start passing to windward ahead of us. I jokingly called, 'Hey Ted, how about throwing me a small line so I can tie my jib down and finish this race?'"

"To my great surprise, he actually did luff his mainsail, drop down alongside and throw me a small line! I'm sure he was aware at the time that if I headed up slightly we would touch sides, and as the windward boat, he would have been disqualified, allowing me to win the race and become the 1946 Southwestern Snipe Champion. I'm pretty sure that he realized that I knew it too!"

"Ted, bless him, was far more concerned with promoting good competition and teaching a young sailor good sportsmanship than he was with winning a race, even a championship race."

"His generous act impressed me much more than his winning the regatta. This fine man taught me yet another valuable lesson, one which I've never forgotten. Unfortunately, during the next fifty years, I've observed far too many "sea lawyers" in sailing competitions. I honestly feel that some of the people believe it's more fun to win by protesting successfully than by crossing the finish line first. I have neither contempt nor pity for these individuals – I simply don't understand them. But I'm saddened to think that today there aren't more sportsmen of Ted's character."[23]

Ted sailing in the 1946 World Competition

Ted became a highly skilled sailor with a knack for racing sailboats, too. He became the District champion five times and won the very competitive National Championships three times; in 1947, 1949, and 1952. He also won the World Championships twice, once in 1947 and again in 1949. His technical knowledge of how to break down and solve problems applied to sailboats and prompted him to author the popular book *Scientific Sailingboat Racing* in 1950.[24] At the time it was the Bible for sailboat racers and was published in multiple languages.

John Rix's autographed copy of *Scientific Sailboat Racing* states "To John Rix – One of those Wichita skippers who are either chewing on my rudder or thumbing their noses at me from ahead—which is the only reason I can win regattas—some of the time –Ted Wells." Ted was a modest man to say the least.

As Ted racked up trophies from regattas, much of it in the form of engraved silverware, a photo in the local paper showed him in front of some of his winnings. This apparently caught the attention of someone from the Internal Revenue Service.

Ted was audited shortly after. During the audit, he was asked about the many trophies that he won. "When did you win that silver tray? How much would you say that was worth? How about that bowl?"

Source: Courtesy of Texas Week, 9/14/1946, published by Raymond Holbrook
Ted with trophies

Ted gladly showed him all the winnings and estimates of their value. Ted knew where this was going as the real question was finally asked; "Why didn't you report those as additional income on your taxes?" So Ted responded with "Ok, if I considered those trophies as income, then let me show you the related expenses I spent to get the trophies."

Ted proceeded to show the auditor his travel expenses, hotel bills, meal receipts, the cost of maintaining his boat and a set of sails that only lasted a couple of years. Obviously, with the expenses far exceeding the value of the trophies he received, he left no doubt that this was a hobby and not a business. That was the last he ever heard from the IRS.

Ted's attendance at regattas was impressive. Not only did he go to regattas around the country, but he also went to regattas in Havana, Monaco, Argentina, and Spain.

The Snipe Class

In March 1931, Bill Crosby, a naval architect, and editor for the *Rudder* magazine, attended a meeting of the Florida West Coast Racing Association in Sarasota, Florida. They asked him to design a class of small racing sailboats suitable for trailering to regattas. Crosby promised to give the proposed class a send-off by designing and publishing plans for building such a boat at home in the July 1931 issue of *Rudder*. The name "Snipe" was chosen following *Rudder's* custom of naming all its designs for seabirds. It was designed to be 15½ ft. long so it could be built with 16 ft. planks. It was easy to haul atop a trailer and could be rigged and launched in a minimum amount of time.

As so many people were poverty stricken the 1930s, a home-built boat was just the thing for inexpensive entertainment. Prior to the advent of air conditioning, visits to the lake were the typical activity for escaping the summer heat. By as early as September of 1931, reports of boats being completed from the plans were received. The first Snipe was built by 14-year-old Jimmy Brown of Pass Christian, Mississippi, who had built the boat with the help of his father. A system of registration and numbering was established so that owners of Snipes living near each other could be put in touch. Snipe Number 1 was assigned to Jimmy Brown.[25]

By May of 1932, 150 boats had been registered, and racing became common as several of the large clubs recognized the Snipe class by giving it its own official starts in the races. Owners began to ask for information on a forming a national class organization for Snipes.

In November of 1932, the Snipe Class International Racing Association (SCIRA) was formed with Dr. Hub E. Isaacks of Dallas, Texas, as the first SCIRA Commodore. Constitution and by-laws were created and the first rulebook was published. By the end of the year there were 250 numbered boats, and Dallas was awarded the first fleet charter; which is still active.

The rules were intended to keep professional designers and builders from gaining an unfair advantage over home builders, so a paragraph was added in the rules for any Snipe to be legal, it must be able to be duplicated by a professional builder for $350, including sails. This was later raised to $450, and then the rule was rewritten to drop the maximum boat price, but instead prohibit the use of exotic and expensive materials. This rule is still in effect today to keep a competitive boat affordable for the nearly everyone.

The first fleet outside the United States was chartered in March of 1933 in Dover, England. In July of 1936, the Snipe class reached the status of world's largest racing class with fleets all over the world. The popularity of the Snipe class continued to grow rapidly with Snipe fleets popping up all over the country. The Wichita Sailing Club originated in 1937 and was assigned as Snipe Fleet #93.

News and developments of the Snipe class were originally published in monthly issues of *Rudder* magazine until the late 1940s. In the mid-1940s, SCIRA began publishing its own monthly newsletter, the Jib Sheet, which was renamed the Snipe Bulletin in the 1950s.[26] For many years, the Snipe Bulletin featured a section called "Well's Wanderings" where Ted Wells gave sailing tips or told stories of his Snipe adventures.

An account from sailor Fracis Seavy tells us about his experience sailing with Ted. "I crewed for Ted in 1946 during the Midwinters at Clearwater, Florida. As we maneuvered before the start, Ted muttered that he was tired of bargers hogging the committee boat end, especially some of the better sailors. With a minute before the start, the bargers were taking positions and Ted was well below them hardening up and advising the approaching boats that they had no rights. After several collisions, they believed Ted and there were wild tacks and gybes to avoid #6025. After racing, while enjoying the grapefruit and Bacardi, the sailors agreed Ted had made his point and on the next day there was plenty of room at the committee boat."[27]

After winning the 1947 US Nationals in Marblehead, Ted didn't know if he'd be able to attend the World races. "I won't know for at least a day or two whether I'll be able to make that trip, I've been three weeks on this trip, spent two at the mid-winter regatta at Clearwater, Fla., and that adds up to five weeks. I think it's about time I spent some time at the plant. We spent nearly three-million dollars developing a four-motor transport plane [Twin-Quad] and we're all set to get it off the ground for the first of many flight tests, which may run well into September. Yes, I'd like to take that trip, but I won't be able to decide for a few days anyway."[28] Ted's wife Marge may have had some influence over this decision as she enjoyed accompanying him to regattas and a trip to Switzerland would be pretty appealing. Ultimately, he did decide to go.

Source: James Rix

1947 National Trophy

First World Championships

A few regattas in the early '40s had participants from other countries making them informal international regattas including one in 1946 at Lake Chautauqua, New York. Sailors from Brazil, Newfoundland, Portugal, and Switzerland participated as well as many from USA fleets. Dr. Martin Dupan, representing Switzerland, was so impressed with the regatta at Chautauqua New York, that he became the initiator for the first world championship to be held outside of the US in Geneva, Switzerland in 1947. This was the first invitational contest just between the national champions from different countries. Since Ted had won the US National regatta, he qualified as the United States representative to the World Championships.

Source: James Rix

1947 World Championship program

In Ted's words, "In 1947, the first world championship was held in Geneva, Switzerland, and it was quite an event. Europe was still recovering from the war, and the Geneva Snipe Fleet had gotten ahold of a small inn out in the country a few miles farther out from Geneva than the yacht club was and had opened it to house the contestants. The inn had been closed all during the war and was completely unfurnished. At the time that Marge and I arrived, the inn had been furnished—with Swiss Army hospital cots—period. No drapes, carpets, chairs—nothing. We were the first ones there and possibly by virtue of that, we had what must have been the deluxe accommodations. The "deluxe" part consisted of having a washbasin with cold running water in the room. The rest of the facilities were in a little room down at the end of the hall, one per floor. I think Marge was taking a pretty dim view of the whole situation when we first arrived, but when everybody showed up, it turned out to be a lot of fun. [29]

In the days before the regatta started, we became aware of the fact that normal wind in Geneva is zero with light puffs, and the boats were rigged accordingly. The natives told us, however, that once in a while "La Bise" would show up. "La Bise" was a north wind which would start out about 30 mph for the first day, would blow for three days at a minimum, and if it were still blowing on the third day, it would blow for three more days with steadily decreasing velocities each day. The boats were all borrowed, and we used the same boat throughout. I immediately moved the mast forward on the boat about 8 inches and slacked off the rigging, much to the disgust of the owner who advised me that the boat was perfectly rigged when I picked it up. We had been very friendly up until that time, but then he became noticeably cool.

"La Bise" showed up the day before the regatta started, and I started winning races. When I had taken first place in all the races, he was very friendly again until the ceremony of turning the boats back in which was to be preceded by putting all the rigging back the way it was when we picked the boats up. This I did in accordance with instructions and then the owner got really mad.

CLASSEMENT DU CHAMPIONNAT DU MONDE

N° de course	2514	5213	5500	5577	5832	5997	5999	6025
Nation	Grande Bretagne	Brésil	Suisse	Norvège	Portugal	Belgique	Canada	Etats-Unis
Régates								
première	8	14	4	6	3	13	7	1
deuxième	8	10	13	3	5	9	6	1
troisième	12	8	4	2	9	11	10	1
quatrième	9	5	2	6	10	12	8	1
cinquième	11	10	9	6	5	2	7	1
Total des points	4493	5036	6067	6640	6021	4390	5581	8000
RANG	11	10	5	3	6	12	8	1

N° de course	6037	6110	6207	6301	6665			
Nations	Espagne	Hongrie	France	Italie	Argentine	Terre Neuve	Canada	Cuba
Régates								
première	14	9	10	5	2			
deuxième	7	13	11	4	2			
troisième	3		5	7	6			
quatrième	7		11	4	3			
cinquième	4		8	3	7			
Total des points	5854	5146	6634	7232				
RANG	7	9	4	2				

BARÈME DES POINTS

1 = 1600	7 = 1156	13 = 784
2 = 1521	8 = 1089	14 = 729
3 = 1444	9 = 1024	15 = 676
4 = 1369	10 = 961	16 = 625
5 = 1296	11 = 900	17 = 576
6 = 1225	12 = 841	18 = 529

Ted's 1947 World Championship score card

Ted beat national champions from 13 countries and won every race. He returned to Wichita as a hero. He was commended by the Board of Commissioners of the City of Wichita for winning both the US National Championships and the World Championships. Newspapers from all over the country gave him great accolades in featured articles, many including the Wichita Eagle covering the story as the headliner on the front page.

World Champion Ted Wells & crew Art Lippit

Ted & Marge Wells after the '47 World Championship

More National and World Championships

Ted didn't have a great experience at the 1948 National Championships in Corpus Christi. During some warm-up sailing in heavy winds prior to the first day of races, he broke his mast. Fortunately, he was able to find another in time for the races. He was doing well in the races and on his way to repeating as the National Champion. He was leading in points and in a position in the final race to win it again. However, his rudder broke and he ended up in finishing last in the race, dropping his final regatta position to fourth. Sometimes luck isn't in your favor.

Source: James Rix

Ted warming up for the '48 Nationals

Since Ted didn't win this competition, he wouldn't get to represent the US in the '48 World Championship.

Ted was able to repeat the victory at the National Championships in Long Beach California to represent the US again at the 1949 World Championships in Larchmont, NY. He handily repeated his victory in these World Championship as well.

WORLD'S CHAMPIONSHIP
SNIPE CLASS INTERNATIONAL RACING ASSOCIATION
1949

LARCHMONT YACHT CLUB
LARCHMONT, N.Y., U.S.A.

RACE SCHEDULE
AUGUST 22-26, 1949

RACE COMMITTEE

ALFRED G. KEESHAN, JR.
RICHARD MAXWELL
GEORGE D. EMMONS
ARTHUR CORKERY
ROBERT MacCALLUM
CLINTON BELL
HAROLD BRAISTED

PROTEST COMMITTEE

ALFRED G. KEESHAN, JR.
DR. H. E. ISAACKS
JOHN T. HAYWARD

Source: James Rix

Program for the 1949 World Championship

After the 1949 world event, SCIRA elected to hold the Worlds only in alternating (odd) years. Ted finished 4th in the '51 National regatta, so he didn't represent the USA in the World Championship in Havana. However, he attended the regatta anyway. Ted had become the ambassador of the Snipe class.

Ted at a social gathering at the Sans Souci night club, Havana

Ted launching boat at the 1952 Nationals

Ted won the National regatta in 1952 at Green Lake Wisconsin, but since it was an even year, there wasn't a world event held.

Ted had a considerable distraction during the 1953 national regatta in Ardmore Oklahoma as will be described later, but he still managed to finish third. While he didn't get to represent the USA at the World Championships in Monaco, he went to that regatta anyway as a spectator.

Program for the 1953 World Championship

Ted just missed out of winning another national regatta in 1954 as he finished second at Mentor Harbor, Ohio. This was the year the SCIRA class organization elected Ted to be the Commodore. Ted finished 6th at the 1955 Nationals in Atlanta, Georgia and dropped to 13th in 1956 at Long

Beach, California, 10th in 1957 in Peoria, Illinois, and 11th in 1958 at Chautauqua Lake, New York. It would appear that Ted had lost his competitive edge, but he came back to finish 3rd in 1959 at Ft. Gibson, Oklahoma and again 3rd in 1960 at Clearwater, Florida. Nevertheless, the number of competitive Snipe sailors had increased since the 1930s and become more experienced and skillful, at least in part from Ted's book and example. Thus the field was more competitive by the 1960s.

In 1962, Ted failed to qualify for the championship fleet of the national regatta and sailed in the consolation fleet named after himself. Ted won this and rumors started floating that perhaps he had sandbagged and intentionally did not qualify for the championship fleet so he could easily win the consolation fleet to get his name on the Wells trophy. However, that would have been uncharacteristic for Ted to ever intentionally sail poorly, let alone in the qualifying series of the nationals.

Eddie Williams

Of course, there are lots of stories from Snipe sailors, but there is another Snipe sailor worth noting; Eddie "Meatball" Williams. Eddie was the owner of the Williams Meat Company in Kansas City. It was Eddie that created a new cut of steak, the Kansas City Strip, later to be called the New York strip by competing meat companies. Some may challenge his claim as the originator of this cut, but there is no refuting evidence one way or the other.

Eddie was a colorful character and he traveled with his personal servant, a black man named BeBop. BeBop would chauffer Eddie to the regatta, launch and rig the boat for him, and then greet him at the dock after the race with a martini in hand. BeBop would hand Eddie the martini and take the boat, unrig it, and put it back on the trailer. Eddie claimed that, "BeBop maintained the finest bar in the country in my car trunk, and it was always open for serious business after the day's racing ended."[30]

Once Eddie got a new Continental convertible and insisted on driving it to a regatta in Miami himself. BeBop, now sitting in the back seat said, "I'm the only colored man with a white chauffeur in Miami!"

Eddie also purchased one of the fast Varalyay boats which were in high demand. Lou Varalyay said that "When we were building Eddie's boat, he kept sending us hams and butter as a hurry-up bribe. Eddie wanted his boat right away, but railway express was as much as the cost of the boat. I checked into air freight which was relatively new. It was also relatively cheap, and TWA agreed to take it." Eddie had his boat the next morning at the airport.

Rules

The SCIRA Board of Governors bought the Snipe plans from *Rudder* magazine in 1948 and SCIRA was incorporated in 1954 making it one of the few racing classes where the class organization owns the design and class rules. Most racing classes are owned and managed by the boat manufacturer which usually control the class rules and often require you to only use their equipment. Having multiple manufacturers keeps the cost to a minimum and allows the class to control the boat construction to ensure older boats remain competitive. In 1958, the Snipe received International Yacht Racing Union (IYRU)'s recognition as an international class. The Snipe class published its own set of rules which controlled construction aspects of the boats as well as racing rules.

Anytime there is competition there are those that try to find ways to gain an advantage. Initially, there were not many rules as it was assumed that the construction of the boats was according to the plans. One method for gaining an advantage was to reduce the weight of the boat as much as possible. The plans called for the hull planks to be ¾" thick. This could be verified by looking at the stern where you could see the bottom planking overlapping the transom. However, some creative racers found a way to lighten their boats and maintain the 3/4" thickness at the stern, by tapering the planks to be thinner everywhere except at the transom.

At a regatta in Southern California, there was a particular Snipe that was incredibly fast. The owner left all the other boats well behind on the first day of races at the regatta. That evening several of the "losers" were hoisting more than a few beers at the clubhouse bar. Naturally, the talk centered on the incredible speed of that boat. Could the boat have been lightened somehow to make it faster? The planks were certainly ¾" thick at the stern, but... could they have been tapered so they were thinner forward of the transom?

After a few more brews, they decided to conduct an unofficial measurement of their own and soon the ad hoc rules committee began their "measurements." They started midship and literally sawed the boat in half, starboard rail to port rail, revealing that indeed all the planks were tapered. They put pushed the two halves back together and neatly placed the cover back in place. The next morning when the owner uncovered his boat, he didn't say a word, but put the cover back on, tied it down, and departed, never to be seen again among the Snipe sailors.[31]

After this incident, there were other protests revolving around plank tapering. After the races of one regatta where a beautiful new varnished boat was suspected of using tapered planks, there was a protest by the sailors, and the fleet measurer took a large wooden drill bit and reluctantly bore a hole through his naturally finished hull to verify its planking thickness. Upon extracting the bit, the hole was open for inspection, and the thickness of the planking was confirmed to be legal. However, the protesting skippers, still not satisfied, requested more holes be drilled at other locations. This idea infuriated the protested skipper to the degree that he grabbed the drill, stormed over to one of the protester's Snipe and screamed, "For every additional test hole drilled in my boat, I will file protests against your boats and drill an equal number of test holes in your hulls." All protests were immediately withdrawn, and he was declared the winner.[32]

Eventually, the rules added a minimum boat weight requirement thus negating any advantage of reducing plank thickness. Ted was never involved in any controversies. He always took the higher ground and followed the intent of the rules. Thus he became well respected and would become the Commodore (president) of SCIRA in 1954 and was the chairman of the rules committee for many years. Over the years, Ted had adopted the suitable nickname "Mr. Snipe" due to his involvement in the class. His challenge as the Rules chair was to keep a fair playing field among many looking for any means that could give them a competitive edge.

As time went on the class rules got more stringent to prevent sailors from gaining an unfair advantage. Today, the first day of a National regatta is spent entirely on measuring the boats. Every boat will be weighed, have its sails measured height, length, and mid-girth along with the size of the sail head and length of individual batons. The mast and boom are measured and the mast weighed along with the center of gravity. The centerboard will be measured and correlated with how far it sticks out the bottom of your boat to verify it is within maximum limits. The rudder is measured; the boom is measured. The latest boat produced by each manufacturer will have several points measured at different stations along the hull. The placement of the mast step will be measured. Even the pitching moment of inertia will be measured. This was a test that Ted developed to keep the construction material evenly distributed throughout the hull layup.

Snipes are extremely soundly built boats that last a long time. Manufacturers can build them lighter and add lead weight to get them to the minimum weight of 381lbs. However, since fiberglass and resin is cheaper than lead, there is incentive to use more fiberglass and less lead. This keeps old boats competitive. My boat is over 25-years old and just as sound as it was when it was built, except for the many dings in the rub rail.

John Rix, my grandfather, built four Snipes. He was a craftsman and built not just the boat hull and deck, but the mast, boom, all the rigging, cleats, bilge pump, and everything from raw materials. He was the head of manufacturing at Cessna and had started working with thermosetting polymers, the new material of the day. One of his creations was called Cessnite, a polyurethane-based epoxy with gravel filler used for forming molds. John Rix, Ted Wells, Francis Lofland, and Harold Gilreath teamed together to build the hull mold for the first fiberglass boats in 1953. For their combined effort in building the mold and laying up fiberglass hulls, each of them got a fiberglass hull shell. The first to come out of the mold in 1954 was #9753. This mold became the launching point for a boat building company, Lofland Boat Works.

Early fiberglass boats weren't competitive with wood boats as the hulls didn't have a lot of stiffness or torsional rigidity as compared to wooden hulls. In subsequent years, other builders of fiberglass Snipes entered the market. One of the major improvements was to build the hull with a fiberglass-foam core system, which made the hulls both stiff and torsionally rigid. But over time, these early foam-core boats would absorb water and become too heavy.

Source: James Rix

Making Cessnite

These improvements finally resulted in a fiberglass hull Snipe winning the 1967 Snipe National Championship, 13 years after the first fiberglass Snipe was built. This ended a reign of championship wins by wooden-hull Snipes that had continued since the first International/National Snipe Championship.[33]

Ted transitioned to a Lofland fiberglass Snipe in 1962 and retired his famous 'Good News III' (#6025). At the National regatta that year in Seattle, Ted's new fiberglass hull didn't pass the measurement. It was too narrow. In order to pass measurement, he took a skill saw and cut down the middle of the deck of his brand new boat and spread it two inches apart. Ted was always adherent to rules.

At one particular national regatta, Ted was serving as the Rules Chair when he noticed someone on a high bluff looking down on the lake from above (where he could see puffs of wind) and tipping off one of the competing boats by radio. Ted seized his own radio and transmitted "To the boat listening to this; I hope you know that receiving guidance from outside the boat is against the rules, and if I find out who you are, you will be disqualified from this race." The problem was he didn't know which boat was listening to the radio and they were smart enough to quit communicating.

The Snipe hull has remained essentially unchanged through the history of the class with only slight changes due to tightening of tolerances and a weight reduction from 425 pounds to 381 pounds. The original 100 square feet of sail area was increased to 116 feet, with the introduction of an overlapping jib which replaced the working jib in 1932. Currently, the sail area is 128 square feet for both the mainsail and overlapping jib. The centerboard has also changed. Early centerboards were made of bronze and went up to the deck level. They were so heavy that crews would swear they were nailed down, and then they'd swear again as they had to raise them for the reaches and runs. Now they are smaller as the centerboard trunks are much lower in the boat and the boards are made out of aluminum, making them much lighter. This accounted for the eventual boat weight reduction in the class rules.

All early Snipes were wood plank hull construction, but starting in the 1950s, fiberglass has taken over as the preferred hull and deck material. This is mostly due to the high maintenance required for wooden boats. Most Snipes are now built by professional builders, but plank and plywood Snipes are still built occasionally and still competitive if the rigging is up to date. Amateurs can build Snipes from plans available from the SCIRA headquarters. Fiberglass Snipes for home finishing may be offered by some builders in various stages of completion. All boats are required to be measured and to carry current SCIRA decals in Snipe class competitions.

Source: Snipe Class International Racing Association

Ted doing research on the self-rescuing holes in the transom

Among other improvements was self-rescuing holes appearing in the transom of the boats in the 70s with floatation built in between an inner and outer hull. This was improved again in the 90's by sealing off the bow and transom completely so the boat would only take on just a little water when capsized. The wood mast and boom was replaced with aluminum in the 60s which was then changed to a small cross section with spreaders that could pre-bend the mast and change the sail shape as conditions dictated.

Currently, over 30,800 Snipes have been registered by SCIRA in 30 countries around the world — making it one of the largest and oldest one-design classes in the world. The Snipe is still one of the top one-design, international racing sailboats in the USA and throughout the World.

Pranks

While Snipe racers take racing seriously, there is definitely a lighter side. The Snipe class Moto is "Serious Racing, Serious Fun," which is certainly applicable. Practical joking is par for course. Fellow competitor Fred Schenck recalls secretly pulling Ted's yellow rudder out of his rudder cover and replacing it with one that was yellow, cut in half. Then on Sunday morning for the third race, Ted pulled his rudder out of the cover, "you can imagine the expression on his face."[34] There are stories of boats found Sunday morning anchored in the middle of the lake or fully rigged floating in a swimming pool. One of these was even done while security was on watch by using a woman as a distraction. There are stories of attaching tin cans to bottoms of boats with fishing line. There are stories of throwing extra hardware in the bottom of boats; seemingly an insignificant thing to do. But nothing is more distracting and worrisome than seeing a screw rolling around in the bottom of your boat. Thoughts immediately jump to, "What did that come off of?" which leads to,

"What's about to fail?" Meanwhile, the racer completely loses focus on the race itself.

At the 1960 Nationals in Clearwater Florida, Eddie returned from the race course with a strange object trailing his boat. When he pulled it from the water, there was a Leopard Ray tied with Eddie's bowline around a screwdriver stabbed through the ray. Eddie proceeded to tell the story of how the ray flew into his boat during the race and scaring the wits out of him and his crew. He let go of the tiller and began trying to get this thing out of his boat and failing that, to kill it. He and his crew began beating and stabbing it with his wooden whisker pole (a boom-like pole used with the jib) until it broke. Then they started beating it with the paddle. That also broke. Finally, he got a screwdriver from his ditty bag and stabbed it to death while leaving screwdriver stab marks all over the cockpit of his wooden boat in the process. For the duration of time that he was dealing with the stingray, his boat was out of control leaving him trailing the fleet too far to recover, so he decided to keep it just to prove his wild story was true. After all, how often does a stingray fly into a boat?[35]

Wichita Sailing Club

With the growth of Snipes fleets around the country, the Wichita Sailing Club on Santa Fe Lake formed in 1937. The photo that follows is from a club race on Santa Fe Lake near Augusta. Ted is in boat 6025; John Rix is skippering 5985 with Ken Rix crewing for him. Ted's sail numbers appear to be faded in this photo, but in reality, they are gold in color. He started a tradition of using gold sail numbers after winning the World Championship. Therefore, the picture was taken sometime after 1947, his first international win.

Source: James Rix

3 Boats on Santa Fe Lake

Source: James Rix

Wichita Sailing Club Clubhouse, 1944

Under Ted's leadership in 1941, the club hosted its first invitational regatta, an event that eventually became the Midwest Championships. These regattas were big events with lots of spectators and press coming to watch and cover it in the newspaper. Typically, it would make the front page of the Social section of the paper. Ted was Commodore of the club a total of six times; in 1941-42, 1948, 1956-57, and 1960.

Like the saying, "You're only good as your competition," the caliber of sailors in the Wichita Sailing Club was tremendous. Ted was a great sailor, but he did not win all the races nor had all the racing seasons' high points every year. Good competition keeps your skills honed. It is a combination of sailing skills: reading the wind, tuning the boat for speed, boat handling, and tactics. And with Mother Nature involved, there's always an element of luck. Racing against the best sailors is what kept everyone excited. Occasionally even the best sailors can be beaten.

Like most other clubs that formed to race Snipes, sailors did not just come to the lake to race. There were always social events on the schedule for regattas, and even in the off-season, there would be picnics, barbecues, dinners, dances (some as formal black-tie affairs) and Christmas parties.

At one time, the club required new members to pass a test of their sailing knowledge before being admitted. There was also a period where all members had to buy a fishing license to meet Fish and Game requirements to gain access to the lake. A Women's Auxiliary was formed in 1943 to help develop an interest in the club. They held rummage sales in the 40s and 50s and used the money for improvements at the lake and for social events.

For a period, Wednesday evening races were quite popular in addition to the weekend races, and it included a potluck dinner afterward in the large screened in patio of the clubhouse. Initially, the club had a hand-cranked hoist for launching boats. It had a pretty good gear ratio for lifting the 400 lb. boats, but it did not have any mechanism to prevent the weight of the boat from spinning the crank handle. So, if anyone accidentally let go of the crank handle, a runaway situation would cause the handle to spin so fast that they dared not try to re-grab it without risking breaking their arm. Several boats got dropped before it was upgraded to a motorized hoist.

One story from Santa Fe Lake involved a drag boat that came into our sailing club dock in the '70s. I have no idea why a drag boat would launch on a lake so small that it could only go in tight circles in the first place, let alone why he wanted to pull up to our sailing club dock. Anyway, he came in fast and then cut the throttle the last second as it approached, slowing quickly right at the dock. However, he didn't realize the consequences that were about to take place: His own sizeable wake came up from behind him and engulfed his boat since his transom was weighted down by an enormous supercharged V-8.

Source: Snipe Class International Racing Association

Ted getting tossed in a pool for winning a regatta

Enough water rolled into the boat, that the added weight was too much for the little freeboard it had. The transom of the boat immediately went to the bottom in about a six-foot depth and leaving the sharp bow sticking out of the water. It happened so fast that he didn't get a chance to kill the engine before it went down. Drawing incompressible fluid into cylinders with lots of moving inertia invariably leaves major damage such as a bent crank. As sailors, it was all we could do to suppress our laughter, but we understood the expense he had just been dealt.

We assisted the unfortunate boater in securing a rope to the bow so he wouldn't have to hire divers to retrieve it if it completely sank. Then he asked to use our hoist to pull it out. Our hoist, rated for about 500 lbs. wouldn't have lifted his engine, let alone the whole boat full of water. He pleaded with us to let him try, but the weight of his boat would only damage our hoist with no chance of pulling his boat out. He ended up having it towed to the other side of the lake where the ramp was that he launched from, dragging it along the bottom of the lake the whole way.

A new reservoir was completed in 1965 west of Wichita near the town of Cheney, Kansas to be used as a water supply for Wichita. A new sailing club, Ninnescah Yacht Club (NYC), formed at that lake and WSC lost a few members to the new club. However, they mostly sailed larger keelboats and didn't draw any of the serious racers away from WSC. They did have races though and one racer at NYC who was consistently winning all the races at Cheney decided to join WSC to race against the Snipe racers on Santa Fe. He purchased a competitive Snipe and in his first race he trailed well behind the fleet. In frustration, he immediately quit the club, sold the Snipe and rejoined NYC. The saying, "You're only as good as your competition," makes it clear that the Wichita Sailing Club racers were very good.

Due to declining membership, the club decided to move to another newly constructed reservoir near Eldorado, Kansas in 1985. Even with his history of racing at Santa Fe, Ted understood the need to move to the larger lake where the club would have more presence, and he voted in favor of moving. Ted also helped secure the site on the new lake by sending a letter to the state from in his capacity as a banker (more on that later). The club didn't want to upset any locals by keeping 'Wichita' in the club name while seeking permission to move next to the town of Eldorado, so it was renamed the Walnut Valley Sailing Club (WVSC). The new lake provided an opportunity for sailing larger boats as well as Snipes, so the club built wet slips to accommodate keelboats. In the long-term, this benefited the club, but didn't help the Snipe Fleet as many members started sailing keelboats instead. By this time, Ted had pretty much retired from racing.

The Snipe Fleet moved to the Ninnescah Sailing Association (renamed from the NYC) at Cheney Reservoir in 2015 and is still hoping to rebuild the fleet as the class is still quite active around the world.

Work Conflicts

After Walter Beech's death in 1950, Olive Ann Beech became the President of Beech Aircraft. She faced power struggles within the company and between her family, the Mellors, and her husband's family. It is difficult to say which threats over control of the company were real and which ones were just perceived. In any event, Olive Ann decided to assert her authority. Her nephew, Frank Hedrick, was loyal to the Mellor family and became instrumental in helping her "clean house."[36]

One of the first to go was R.K. Beech, Walter's own brother, who was a corporate vice president. He didn't resign but was moved to a position of considerably lower rank within the company. The demotion of R.K. Beech left Walter's nephew, Ed Burns next in line. Frank Hedrick called him into his office and asked him point blank where his loyalties lay. Ed, a young employee, previously in a low-level position, agreed to remain loyal to Olive Ann and thus kept his job.

According to Ed's son Walter, "For me, growing up in the Beech family was always very confusing, and more than a little intimidating. There was this hierarchy of power that was always in play. Olive Ann of course sat at the top of the mountain. Hedrick paid obeisance to her, but all the while bristled that she stood above him, blocking his path to the top. He took his frustration out, to some extent, on my dad by keeping him under his thumb. Somehow I always knew that all this grew out of the family power hierarchy within Beech Aircraft. I was aware from an early age that people could "disappear" from the family – as R.K. Beech did, and as Bill Beech did later—and that once they were gone, they were rarely ever spoken of again. When I think about it all now, it really was kind of strange."[37]

Although Ted was unlikely to have been interested in running the company, it became apparent that tensions between he and Olive Ann were increasing. Publically, Olive Ann said she did not like Ted spending time sailing and thought he needed to spend more time focused on the company. In 1953, Olive Ann sent a plane down to pick him up from the Snipe National regatta in Ardmore, Oklahoma for an "emergency meeting" back in Wichita.

Ted left the regatta, attended the meeting which amounted to Olive Ann telling him "I think that you ought to have all the free time you need for your interests. We accept your resignation."[38] Ted signed the resignation letter and immediately returned to the regatta. Fellow sailors were shocked hearing the news that he was no longer associated with Beech Aircraft and we can only imagine the distraction it would have had for Ted who remained in the race.

No one really knows the real reasons that led to Olive Ann's termination of Ted. One theory is that Olive Ann was threatened by Ted since he was good friends with Walter and she took an opportunity to force him out. According to Ted, "There was a difference in philosophies on how to run the organization. I felt the executives should do longer range planning and not [work on] the daily bonfires. If they want to take time off to go someplace else, I think they ought to be able to do it. Some didn't agree with that."[39]

After Ted left, he started doing consulting work for Lear Jet and McDonnell, and it was no secret that he wanted to spend more time racing Snipe sailboats anyway. It was just as likely that he considered Beech Aircraft as interfering with his sailing. Ted had always had the independent streak that had been there when he flew to Princeton and he certainly didn't need the money.

Olive Ann became very good at exercising authority, perhaps driven by being a woman leader at a time when she was constantly challenged by men seeking to further their own authority. The Beechcraft name was emblazoned on everything. Olive Ann wanted every instrument in the instrument panel to have the Beechcraft name on it. This was a silk-screening challenge for the smallest instruments. The rudder pedals on the T-34 were in the shape of the Beech 'B' logo. The Navy, however, didn't like it and wanted Beech to remove the Beech 'B' from them. Olive Ann held her ground and defiantly stated, "If you want my airplanes, then you'll get them with the Beech 'B' rudder pedals." Needless to say, they were delivered to the Navy with the Beech 'B' rudder pedals.

Ted eventually retired from the aircraft industry. Bob Langiwater, a banker and fellow member of the Wichita Sailing Club, talked Ted into making an offer for the Central Bank & Trust financial institution which was looking for a buyer. Ted made an offer but was declined. Ted didn't bother with a counter offer and for the most part forgot about it. It turns out that no one else showed any interest and a year later Central Bank & Trust came back to Ted and accepted his original offer. Ted purchased 90% of the controlling stock for 12 million dollars. He became the principal owner and chairman of the board and his investment grew to 105 million before his interview in 1988.

And of course, Ted continued to race Snipes. The last regatta he participated in was the 1986 National Master's regatta hosted by the Atlanta Yacht Club when he was 79.

Although Ted and Marge had no children and were financially well off (they were the heirs to Marge's wealthy family and Ted had had a very successful career), Ted was very frugal. He spent as little as possible maintaining his boat almost to the point of allowing it to go into complete disrepair. He expected his crew that traveled with him to regattas to pay for their own lodging and meals even though traditionally skippers would take care of all their crew's expenses associated with the regatta.

A story from fellow sailor Lowry Lamb illustrates this. "A number of years ago, a meeting of District-Two Snipe sailors was held in Oklahoma City. Since Ted was to fly in from Wichita, the meeting was held in the restaurant at the airport. Ted was well known for his penny-pinching ways. So, Bill Kilpatrick and the others already there, decided they would pick up the tab. Ted was on schedule, so the meeting only took a short time. When the meeting ended, no one made a move to leave. They knew Ted would have to leave soon and they just waited to see what would happen. After a bit of squirming, Ted finally put down a quarter and said, "That should take care of my coffee."[40]

Ted was a gentleman though. He always competed with the most sportsman-like manner, but he had no tolerance for what he considered to be foolish questions and declined to give any information that he felt any sailor should know or could find in the rule book. He would simply tell them to look it up themselves. He had, after all, written the bible on the subject of sailboat racing.

Final Chapter

Source: James Rix

Ted & Marge at party

At 84 years old, Ted passed away in September of 1991. Between the relationships he made in the aircraft industry, the sailing community, and his banking associates, his funeral service was standing room only. However, today the Beech Aircraft Company only acknowledges Walter and Olive Ann Beech for being the founders of Beech Aircraft. All the pictures, buildings, and memorabilia at the Beech factory are in Walter or Olive Ann Beech's name (I.e. Walter Beech Hall, Olive Ann Gallery, etc.). There isn't even a mention of Ted Wells with the display of the Staggerwing serial #3 in the lobby of the delivery center. Most books and histories about Beech Aircraft contain very little about—or no mention of—the man who designed some of the most successful aircraft in history.

Ted's championship boat 'Good News III' (#6025) is on display in the small-boat collection at the Mystic Seaport Museum in Connecticut. One of his old cotton main sails with gold numbers and chevrons designating World Champion status is on display at the Ninnescah Sailing Association clubhouse at Cheney Lake.

In 2008, the Wichita Snipe Fleet #93 hosted a Ted Wells memorial regatta. At the awards ceremony, longtime friends of Ted and Marge shared some stories of the legendary sailor and then the regatta awards presented were some of the many trophies that Ted had accumulated over the years that were picked up from his estate sale. Unfortunately, they didn't include the World Championship trophies.

Beech Aircraft went through several transitions after Olive Ann Beech sold the company to Raytheon; changing the name to Raytheon Aircraft, to spinning off the name Hawker Beechcraft. Then it was the sale to Goldman Sacks and the restructured Beechcraft Company emerging after going through bankruptcy only to be purchased by Textron, the parent company of Cessna Aircraft and the merged Beech/Cessna companies being named Textron Aviation.

The lakes north of the Beech facility were built as a water source for fire protection of the mostly wooden buildings at Plant 1. You can see a water tower in the early facility photograph. However, it also served as a dual purpose as Olive Ann had gifted the property to the employees through the employee's club. These lakes hosted many activities for employees including baseball diamonds, rifle range, several picnic sites with playground equipment, docks for fishing and boating, and a radio-controlled airplane park. As a result of the company's financial difficulties encountered prior to bankruptcy, the company managed to gain title of the lake property and sold it in two separate sales for the north and south lakes.

Since the word 'Beechcraft' had been painted on the roof of Plant 1, it has been identified by the FAA as a navigation aid for the Beech Field airport. After parent company Raytheon renamed Beech Aircraft to 'Raytheon Aircraft', they wanted to paint over the Beechcraft on the roof, but the FAA wouldn't allow it. The same thing happened when Beechcraft was bought by Textron and the company was renamed Textron Aviation.

The fact that a name associated with Beech Aircraft remains on the roof greatly pleases many old-time Beechcrafters who value the history of Beech and its tradition of building some of the finest airplanes in the world. Who would have dreamed when Ted Wells first built an airplane in his parent's garage the incredible amount of aircraft development that would occur in such a short amount of time? In his retirement, Ted and Marge Wells took a vacation and flew from New York to Paris in a Concorde at Mach 2.

Whether or not he is remembered as part of Beech Aircraft's official corporate history, Ted Wells and the airplanes he designed will always be a part of aeronautics history as perhaps the best aircraft designer during air flight's pioneering era and a world-class sailor of great skill.

Sun rising through Beechcraft tunnel

About the Author

James Rix has been an avionics certification engineer for Textron Aviation (Beech Aircraft) for 32 years. James may be the last current employee of Beech that was a personal acquaintance of Ted Wells. James is also an aircraft history enthusiast with a long family history in aviation. His grandfather, John Rix, grew up watching early pioneers, including DeBlériot, fly at the Hendon Aerodrome outside of London. He worked with De Bothezat on a helicopter that flew in 1922. Many historians consider this to be the first successful helicopter. John created the tooling department at Cessna for building the gliders that dropped troops in Belgium in WWII. He became the head of Cessna manufacturing, and later was a manufacturing consultant for Beech Aircraft.

James' father, Ken Rix, worked at Beech Aircraft in preliminary design. He then went to Lear Jet as Chief of Advanced Design and left there to help startup an aviation related company, Aerospace Systems and Controls.

James is also a third generation Snipe sailboat racer and grew up crewing with and competing against Ted Wells in his youth in the Wichita Sailing Club. James finished 5th in the Wells fleet in the 2000 US Nationals, a trophy named after Ted for the winner of the consolation fleet of the US Nationals.

Relentlessly Creative Books™ offers an exciting new publishing option for authors. Our "middle-path publishing" approach includes many of the advantages of both traditional publishing and self-publishing without the drawbacks. For more information and a complete online catalog of our books, please visit us online.

RelentlesslyCreativeBooks.com
books@relentlesslycreative.com

End Notes

1 http://history.nasa.gov/SP-4406/chap1.html

2 Ted Wells interview by Ed Phillips

3 Omaha newspaper

4 Princeton History web page

5 Wichita Eagle May 30, 1982

6 Wichita Eagle May 26, 1994

7 http://www.aviation-history.com/travelair/mystery.html

8 Historical Development of Aircraft Flutter, Nov 1981

9 History of Flight Flutter Testing, 1975

10 https://en.wikipedia.org/wiki/Curtiss-Wright_CW-12

11 Eagle Beacon, April 10, 1932

12 http://bit.ly/2Gn7TtX_AeroPhotos

13 http://bit.ly/2BxFQnT_Wells_Manual

14 Beech Log April 16, 1943

15 Letter from Max Eaton, 11-16-96

16 http://bit.ly/2nmOHDZ_AviationHistory

17 http://www.wingsoverkansas.com/murphy/a645/

18 https://en.wikipedia.org/wiki/Beechcraft_Model_34

19 http://www.wingsoverkansas.com/murphy/a645/

20 Recollection from Virgil Fisher

21 Snipe Bulletin Spring 2011

22 Scientific Sailboat Racing

23 *Half the World are Squirrels and the Rest are Nuts*, Pierre Havre

24 http://bit.ly/2FpeCSS_Scientific_sailboat_racing

25 https://snipeusa.com/about/the-snipe-class-history/

26 ibid

27 Snipe Tales 1996

28 Wichita Eagle July 19, 1947

29 Snipe Bulletin Sep. 1981

30 Snipe Tales 1996

31 ibid

32 ibid

33 Snipe Bulletin 75th Anniversary Edition

[34] Snipe Tales 1996

[35] ibid

[36] The Barnstormer and the Lady, Dennis Farney

[37] ibid

[38] ibid

[39] Ted Wells interview by Ed Phillips

[40] Snipe Tales 1996